I0844433

Table Of Contents

Table of Contents

Chapter 1: Introduction to Passive Income Mastery

The Benefits of Passive Income

In today's fast-paced digital world, more and more people are seeking ways to make money online. Whether you dream of financial freedom, extra income, or the flexibility to work from anywhere, passive income has become a popular solution. In this subchapter, we will delve into the numerous benefits of passive income and how it can transform your financial situation.

One of the primary advantages of passive income is that it allows you to break free from the traditional 9-to-5 grind. Instead of trading hours for dollars, passive income streams work for you around the clock. Whether you're sleeping, on vacation, or spending time with loved ones, your passive income continues to grow. This newfound freedom gives you the opportunity to live life on your own terms and pursue your passions without being tied down by a traditional job.

Another benefit of passive income is the potential for unlimited earning potential. Unlike a fixed salary, passive income is not limited by a set amount of hours worked or a specific job title. With the right strategies and dedication, your passive income can grow exponentially over time. It provides you with the opportunity to create multiple streams of income, diversifying your revenue sources and reducing the risk of relying on a single source of income.

Passive income also offers a sense of financial security. By diversifying your income streams, you are not solely dependent on a single job or client. This financial stability provides peace of mind and the confidence to pursue your dreams without the constant worry of financial instability.

Furthermore, passive income allows you to leverage your skills and interests to generate income. Whether you're a talented writer, a social media guru, or a creative designer, there are countless opportunities to monetize your skills online. Whether it's starting a blog, creating and selling digital products, managing social media accounts, or freelancing, passive income enables you to turn your hobbies and expertise into profitable ventures.

Lastly, passive income provides a pathway to financial independence and the ability to build wealth. By consistently investing in passive income streams, you can create a reliable source of income that grows over time. This can lead to long-term financial stability, early retirement, or the ability to pursue your dreams without financial constraints.

In conclusion, passive income offers a multitude of benefits for individuals looking to make money online. It provides freedom, unlimited earning potential, financial security, the ability to leverage your skills, and a pathway to financial independence. Whether you're interested in blogging for profit, e- commerce, creating digital products, social media management, podcasting, online courses, or freelancing, passive income mastery is the ultimate guide to help you achieve your financial goals and live life on your own terms.

Understanding the Online Passive Income Landscape

In today's digital age, there are countless opportunities to make money online. The online passive income landscape offers a wide array of options for individuals who are looking to generate income from the comfort of their own homes. Whether you're interested in blogging for profit, e-commerce, creating and selling digital products, social media management and marketing, podcasting, creating online courses, or freelancing, this subchapter aims to provide you with a comprehensive understanding of the online passive income landscape.

One of the most popular methods of generating passive income online is through blogging for profit. Blogging allows individuals to share their expertise or interests with a wide audience while monetizing their content through various channels such as affiliate marketing, sponsored posts, or selling digital products. We will explore the strategies and techniques that successful bloggers use to generate a substantial income from their blogs.

E-commerce and dropshipping have also gained immense popularity in recent years. With the rise of platforms like Shopify and Amazon, starting an online store has become more accessible than ever. We will delve into the world of e-commerce and dropshipping, discussing how to source products, build a brand, and effectively market your online store to maximize profits.

Creating and selling digital products is another lucrative avenue for generating passive income online. Whether it's e-books, online courses, stock photography, or design templates, there is a vast market for digital products. We will explore the different types of digital products you can create and provide tips on how to market and sell your creations effectively.

Social media management and marketing have become essential skills in the online business world. With billions of users on platforms like Facebook, Instagram, and Twitter, businesses are constantly looking for skilled individuals to manage their social media presence. We will discuss the strategies and techniques that social media managers use to grow their clients' online presence and generate income through social media management.

Podcasting and monetizing audio content have also emerged as a popular form of passive income. We will explore the world of podcasting, discussing how to start a podcast, grow your audience, and monetize your content through sponsorships, advertising, and merchandise sales.

Creating and selling online courses has become a booming industry. If you have expertise in a particular field, creating an online course can be an excellent way to generate passive income. We will provide insights into the process of creating, marketing, and selling online courses effectively.

Lastly, we will explore the world of freelancing and online service-based businesses. Whether you're a writer, graphic designer, programmer, or virtual assistant, freelancing allows you to leverage your skills to generate income on your terms. We will discuss various freelancing platforms, pricing strategies, and how to build a successful online service-based business.

By the end of this subchapter, you will have a comprehensive understanding of the online passive income landscape, allowing you to choose the path that aligns best with your interests and skills. Whether you decide to start a blog, launch an e-commerce store, create digital products, manage social media accounts, start a podcast, create online courses, or offer freelance services, this subchapter will equip you with the knowledge and tools to succeed in the online business world.

Chapter 2: Make Money with Online Passive Income

Exploring Different Passive Income Streams

In today's fast-paced digital world, there are countless opportunities to generate passive income online. Whether you're looking to earn a little extra cash on the side or want to completely replace your current income, exploring various passive income streams can provide you with the financial freedom you desire. This subchapter will delve into the numerous possibilities available to you, catering to individuals who want to make money in a range of niches.

One popular avenue to explore is making money with online passive income. This encompasses a wide range of possibilities, including affiliate marketing, creating and selling online courses, and utilizing advertising platforms such as Google AdSense. Through these methods, you can earn a passive income by generating revenue from your website or blog as visitors engage with your content.

Another lucrative niche is blogging for profit. With the right strategy and quality content, you can monetize your blog through sponsored posts, affiliate marketing, and even selling your own products or services. This subchapter will provide you with essential tips and techniques to transform your blog into a profitable venture.

E-commerce and dropshipping have also gained immense popularity in recent years. By setting up an online store and leveraging platforms like Shopify, you can sell physical products without worrying about inventory management or shipping. We will guide you through the process of finding profitable niches, sourcing products, and implementing effective marketing strategies to ensure success.

Creating and selling digital products is another fantastic passive income stream. Whether it's eBooks, online courses, or software, digital products can generate consistent revenue long after they are created. We will explore the steps involved in creating and marketing these products, helping you tap into this profitable market.

Social media management and marketing have become essential for businesses of all sizes. By leveraging your social media skills, you can offer services to clients and generate a steady income stream. This subchapter will provide insights on how to build a successful social media management business and attract high-paying clients.

Podcasting and monetizing audio content have also gained significant traction. We will delve into the world of podcasting, guiding you through the steps to create engaging content, attract a dedicated audience, and monetize your podcast through sponsorships and advertising.

Freelancing and online service-based businesses are ideal for those with specific skills and expertise. This subchapter will explore the various freelancing opportunities available, such as graphic design, writing, programming, and more. We will equip you with the knowledge to market your services effectively and build a thriving online business.

No matter your interests or skills, this subchapter will provide you with a comprehensive guide to exploring different passive income streams. By diversifying your income sources and leveraging the power of the internet, you can achieve financial independence and live life on your terms.

Investing in Dividend Stocks and Bonds

In the world of passive income, one of the most reliable and time-tested strategies is investing in dividend stocks and bonds. This subchapter will explore how you can make money by leveraging these investment vehicles, catering to the diverse audience of people who are eager to make money through various online avenues.

Dividend stocks are shares of companies that distribute a portion of their profits to shareholders on a regular basis. These payouts, known as dividends, can be an excellent source of passive income. By investing in dividend stocks, you become a part-owner of the company and are entitled to a share of its earnings. This means that as the company grows and generates profits, your investment also grows, leading to potential capital appreciation alongside regular dividend payments.

On the other hand, bonds are fixed-income securities that represent a loan given by an investor to a borrower, typically a government or a corporation. Bonds pay interest to investors at fixed intervals, providing a steady stream of income. They are considered less risky than stocks, making them an attractive option for those seeking stability in their passive income endeavors.

Investing in dividend stocks and bonds requires careful research and analysis. It is crucial to diversify your portfolio by spreading your investments across different industries and asset classes. This strategy helps mitigate risk and maximize potential returns.

For individuals in the niche of e-commerce and dropshipping, investing in dividend stocks and bonds can be an excellent way to diversify income streams. By generating passive income through investments, you can supplement your online business earnings and create a more stable financial foundation.

Similarly, for those involved in creating and selling digital products, dividend stocks and bonds offer an opportunity to build a passive income stream that complements your online sales. By investing in these assets, you can create a reliable source of income that is not solely dependent on your digital product sales.

No matter which online avenue you choose to pursue, incorporating dividend stocks and bonds into your investment strategy can provide a steady stream of passive income. Whether you are a blogger, social media manager, podcaster, or online course creator, investing in dividend stocks and bonds can help you achieve financial security and freedom.

In conclusion, investing in dividend stocks and bonds is a tried and tested strategy for making money passively. By exploring this investment avenue, you can diversify your income streams and create a more stable financial future. Whether you are engaged in e-commerce, blogging, digital product creation, or any other online business, incorporating dividend stocks and bonds into your investment portfolio can help you achieve your financial goals.

Real Estate Investments and Rental Properties

For those looking to diversify their income streams and generate passive income, real estate investments and rental properties can be an excellent avenue to explore. In this subchapter, we will delve into the world of real estate investing and its potential for making money online.

Real estate investments offer a unique opportunity to build wealth over time, and with the advent of online platforms, it has become increasingly accessible for individuals seeking to make money.
Whether you are interested in residential properties, commercial spaces, or vacation rentals, there are various avenues to explore within the real estate market.

One popular method for making money online through real estate is by investing in rental properties. Owning a rental property allows you to generate passive income by renting out the space to tenants. With the right property and management strategies, you can create a steady stream of cash flow that requires minimal effort on your part.

To begin your journey into real estate investing, it is essential to conduct thorough research and due diligence. Understand the local market trends, analyze potential rental yields, and identify target demographics. This knowledge will enable you to make informed decisions and maximize your returns.

When it comes to managing rental properties, leveraging online platforms can streamline the process and minimize the time and effort required. Utilize property management software to automate tasks such as rent collection, maintenance requests, and tenant screenings. This will free up your time to focus on growing your real estate portfolio and expanding your income streams.

Additionally, consider implementing digital marketing strategies to attract potential tenants. Leverage social media platforms, create engaging content, and optimize your online presence to reach a wider audience. By harnessing the power of the internet, you can effectively market your rental properties and ensure a consistent flow of tenants.

Real estate investments and rental properties offer a tangible and reliable way to generate passive income online. However, it is crucial to approach this venture with careful planning, research, and a solid strategy. By understanding the market, leveraging online tools, and implementing effective marketing tactics, you can create a lucrative real estate portfolio and achieve financial success.

In conclusion, real estate investments and rental properties present an exciting opportunity for individuals looking to make money online. Whether you are already involved in other online passive income ventures or are looking to diversify your income streams, real estate can offer stable and consistent returns. By understanding the market, utilizing online platforms, and implementing effective management and marketing strategies, you can achieve financial freedom and create a sustainable source of passive income.

Peer-to-Peer Lending Platforms

Peer-to-peer lending platforms have revolutionized the way people can make money online. These platforms provide an opportunity for individuals to lend money directly to others, cutting out traditional financial institutions and allowing for higher returns on investment.

For those interested in making money through online passive income, peer-to-peer lending offers a unique and profitable avenue. With traditional investments such as stocks and bonds yielding low returns, peer-to-peer lending provides an alternative option that can generate consistent income. By lending money to borrowers, individuals can earn interest on their investment, often at rates higher than what can be achieved through traditional banking methods.

Blogging for profit is another popular niche for those seeking to make money online. Peer-to-peer lending platforms can be an excellent addition to a blogger's revenue streams. By discussing the benefits and risks of peer-to-peer lending on their blog, bloggers can attract a new audience interested in alternative investment opportunities. As an affiliate marketer, bloggers can also earn commissions by referring their readers to reputable peer-to-peer lending platforms.

E-commerce and dropshipping have skyrocketed in popularity in recent years. As an online business owner, integrating peer-to-peer lending into your business model can be highly beneficial. By lending money to small businesses or entrepreneurs looking to expand their inventory, you can support their growth while earning interest on your investment.

Creating and selling digital products is another lucrative way to make money online. Whether it's an e- book, online course, or software, digital products are in high demand. By utilizing peer-to-peer lending platforms, you can finance the development and production of your digital products while earning passive income from the interest generated.

Social media management and marketing professionals can also benefit from incorporating peer-to- peer lending platforms into their business strategies. By promoting these platforms to their clients, social media managers can help them diversify their investment portfolios and potentially increase their returns.

Podcasting and monetizing audio content have become increasingly popular in recent years. By discussing the benefits and risks of peer-to-peer lending on their podcasts, hosts can attract listeners interested in maximizing their online passive income opportunities.

Creating and selling online courses is a profitable niche within the online business world. By including a section on peer-to-peer lending in their courses, entrepreneurs can provide their students with valuable information on alternative investment options.

Freelancers and online service-based businesses can also benefit from peer-to-peer lending platforms. By lending money to fellow freelancers or small business owners, freelancers can support their peers while earning interest on their investment.

In conclusion, peer-to-peer lending platforms offer a lucrative opportunity for individuals looking to make money online. Whether you're interested in online passive income, blogging for profit, e- commerce and dropshipping, creating and selling digital products, social media management and marketing, podcasting and monetizing audio content, creating and selling online courses, or freelancing and online service-based businesses, peer-to-peer lending can be a valuable addition to your income streams.

Chapter 3: Blogging for Profit

Choosing a Profitable Niche for Your Blog

In today's digital era, making money online has become a popular goal for many people. Whether you are looking to escape the nine-to-five grind or simply want to supplement your income, creating a profitable blog can be the key to financial freedom. However, with so many niches to choose from, it can be overwhelming to decide which one is right for you. In this subchapter, we will explore various niches that have the potential to generate passive income and help you make an informed decision.

One of the most lucrative niches is "Make Money with Online Passive Income." This niche focuses on teaching others how to generate passive income streams through various online methods. Whether it's affiliate marketing, selling digital products, or building an e-commerce empire, this niche offers endless opportunities for growth and financial success. By sharing your knowledge and experiences, you can inspire others to achieve their own financial freedom.

Another popular niche is "Blogging for Profit." In this digital age, blogging has become a powerful platform for individuals to share their passions and generate income. By selecting a niche that aligns with your interests and expertise, you can create engaging content that attracts a loyal audience.

From sponsored posts to affiliate marketing, blogging offers numerous avenues for monetization.

E-commerce and dropshipping are also highly profitable niches. With the rise of online shopping, many entrepreneurs have found success by setting up their own online stores. By sourcing products from suppliers and leveraging various marketing strategies, you can create a thriving e-commerce business that generates passive income.

If you have a talent for creating digital products, consider the niche of "Creating and Selling Digital Products." From e-books to online courses, digital products have become increasingly popular due to their low production costs and high profit margins. By sharing your expertise and packaging it into a digital product, you can create a passive income stream that generates revenue while you sleep.

Social media management and marketing is another niche worth exploring. With the ever-growing popularity of social media platforms, businesses are constantly seeking experts to manage their online presence. By offering social media management services, you can help businesses build their brand and increase their online visibility while earning a steady income.

Podcasting and monetizing audio content have also gained traction in recent years. If you have a passion for audio content and enjoy engaging with an audience, this niche could be perfect for you. By creating valuable and entertaining podcasts, you can attract sponsors and advertisers, turning your passion into a profitable venture.

Creating and selling online courses is yet another profitable niche. With the increasing demand for online education, individuals are willing to pay for valuable knowledge and skills. If you have expertise in a specific field, consider creating an online course and sharing your knowledge with others while earning a passive income.

Finally, freelancing and online service-based businesses offer a wide range of opportunities. From graphic design to content writing, there is a high demand for skilled freelancers in various industries. By offering your services online, you can build a client base and generate income on your terms.

In conclusion, choosing a profitable niche for your blog is crucial for achieving online success. By exploring niches such as make money with online passive income, blogging for profit, e-commerce and dropshipping, creating and selling digital products, social media management and marketing, podcasting, creating and selling online courses, and freelancing and online service-based businesses, you can find a niche that aligns with your interests and skills. Remember, success in the online world comes from passion, dedication, and providing value to your audience.

Setting Up and Designing Your Blog

In today's digital age, having a blog is one of the most effective ways to generate passive income and make money online. Whether you are interested in making money through affiliate marketing, sponsored content, or selling your own products, setting up and designing your blog is the first step towards achieving your financial goals. In this subchapter, we will guide you through the process of creating a successful blog that aligns with your niche and target audience.

When starting a blog, it is crucial to choose a niche that you are passionate about and that has potential for profitability. This book caters to a wide range of niches, including making money with online passive income, blogging for profit, e-commerce and dropshipping, creating and selling digital products, social media management and marketing, podcasting and monetizing audio content, creating and selling online courses, and freelancing and online service-based businesses. Once you have identified your niche, you can begin the process of setting up your blog.

The first step in setting up your blog is to choose a domain name and a hosting provider. Your domain name should be catchy, memorable, and relevant to your niche. Additionally, it is essential to select a reliable hosting provider that offers excellent uptime and customer support.

After setting up your blog, it is time to design it in a way that attracts and engages your target audience. Choose a visually appealing and user-friendly theme that complements your niche. Customize your blog's layout, colors, and fonts to reflect your brand identity. Make sure your blog is mobile-friendly, as an increasing number of users access the internet from their smartphones and tablets.

When designing your blog, it is crucial to consider the user experience. Ensure that your blog is easy to navigate, with clear categories and tags that help visitors find the content they are looking for. Use high-quality images and videos to enhance the visual appeal of your blog posts.

Lastly, optimize your blog for search engines by incorporating relevant keywords into your content. This will help increase your blog's visibility in search engine results and attract organic traffic.
Additionally, regularly update your blog with fresh and valuable content to keep your readers engaged and coming back for more.

Setting up and designing your blog is an exciting and essential step towards making money online. By following the guidelines outlined in this subchapter, you will be well on your way to building a successful and profitable blog in your chosen niche.

Creating High-Quality Content to Attract Readers

In the vast world of online money-making opportunities, one thing remains constant: content is king. Whether you're delving into the realms of online passive income, blogging for profit, e-commerce and dropshipping, creating and selling digital products, social media management and marketing, podcasting and monetizing audio content, creating and selling online courses, or freelancing and online service-based businesses, the key to success lies in creating high-quality content that captivates and engages readers.

But what exactly does high-quality content entail? It goes beyond simply stringing together words and sentences. It involves understanding your target audience and addressing their needs, wants, and pain points. It means providing valuable information, actionable tips, and unique insights that your readers won't find elsewhere. It's about being authentic, relatable, and trustworthy.

To start creating high-quality content, you must first identify your niche and target audience. What are you passionate about? What expertise or knowledge do you possess that can benefit others? Once you've determined your niche, conduct thorough research to understand the needs, desires, and challenges faced by your target audience. This will enable you to tailor your content to their specific needs and interests.

Next, focus on developing a unique voice and style that sets you apart from the competition. Inject your personality into your writing, and don't be afraid to share personal anecdotes and experiences. This will help you build a genuine connection with your readers, fostering trust and loyalty.

Remember, high-quality content is not only about written articles or blog posts. Explore different mediums such as videos, podcasts, infographics, and social media posts to diversify your content offerings and reach a wider audience.

Consistency is another crucial aspect of creating high-quality content. Set a schedule and stick to it. Whether you commit to posting once a week or once a day, ensure that you consistently deliver valuable content to your readers. This will not only keep them engaged but also improve your search engine rankings, leading to increased visibility and organic traffic.

Lastly, always strive for improvement. Continuously seek feedback from your readers and analyze your content's performance. Use tools like Google Analytics to track metrics such as page views, bounce rates, and time spent on your site. This data will help you identify trends, understand what resonates with your audience, and refine your content strategy accordingly.

Creating high-quality content is an ongoing process that requires dedication, creativity, and a deep understanding of your audience. By consistently delivering valuable, engaging, and unique content, you will attract readers, build a loyal following, and ultimately achieve your goal of making money online.

Monetizing Your Blog with Advertisements and Affiliate Marketing

In today's digital age, there are countless opportunities to make money online. Whether you are a blogger, e-commerce entrepreneur, or someone looking to tap into the world of passive income, monetizing your blog with advertisements and affiliate marketing is a fantastic way to generate revenue. This subchapter will guide you through the process of making money through these lucrative avenues.

Advertisements are a tried and tested method of monetizing your blog. By displaying ads on your website, you can earn money whenever visitors click on these ads or make a purchase through them. There are various advertising networks available, such as Google AdSense, Media.net, and Amazon Associates, that allow you to easily integrate ads into your blog. You will learn how to optimize ad placement, choose relevant ad formats, and drive traffic to increase your ad revenue.

Affiliate marketing is another powerful way to monetize your blog. By partnering with companies and promoting their products or services through your blog, you can earn a commission for every sale or lead generated through your affiliate links. This subchapter will teach you how to choose the right affiliate programs, effectively promote products, and build a loyal audience that trusts your recommendations.

For those with an e-commerce or dropshipping business, integrating advertisements and affiliate marketing into your blog can further boost your revenue. You will discover how to strategically place ads and create engaging content that seamlessly incorporates affiliate links, driving traffic to your store and increasing conversions.

Additionally, this subchapter will explore other online income streams, such as creating and selling digital products, social media management and marketing, podcasting, creating online courses, freelancing, and online service-based businesses. You will learn how to leverage your blog's audience and establish yourself as an expert in your niche, allowing you to successfully monetize your skills and knowledge.

Whether you are a seasoned blogger or just starting out, "Monetizing Your Blog with Advertisements and Affiliate Marketing" is a must-read for anyone looking to make money online. With step-by-step guidance and practical tips, this subchapter will equip you with the knowledge and tools to turn your blog into a profitable venture. Start your journey towards passive income mastery today!

Building an Email List and Leveraging it for Profit

In today's digital age, where making money online has become a popular and lucrative endeavor, one of the most powerful tools at your disposal is building an email list. An email list is a collection of email addresses that individuals willingly provide, allowing you to directly communicate with them and nurture a relationship of trust and credibility. In this subchapter, we will explore the importance of building an email list and how to leverage it for profit, regardless of your niche.

Whether you are interested in making money with online passive income, blogging for profit, e- commerce and dropshipping, creating and selling digital products, social media management and marketing, podcasting and monetizing audio content, creating and selling online courses, or freelancing and online service-based businesses, an email list is crucial for your success.

Why is an email list so valuable? Simply put, it gives you direct access to your target audience. Unlike other platforms that are subject to algorithms and ever-changing rules, an email list allows you to bypass these limitations and reach your subscribers directly. You have the power to send personalized messages, exclusive offers, and valuable content that will keep your audience engaged and eager to hear from you.

To build an email list, you need to offer something of value in exchange for your audience's email addresses. This could be a free e-book, a helpful guide, a discount code, or exclusive access to content. By providing something enticing, you encourage people to willingly share their contact information, enabling you to establish a connection and build trust.

Once you have built an email list, it's time to leverage it for profit. This can be done through various strategies such as email marketing campaigns, promoting your products or services, affiliate marketing, or even selling advertising space within your emails. By nurturing your list and consistently providing value, you can convert subscribers into paying customers or clients, generating a passive income stream that continues to grow over time.

Remember, building an email list is not a one-time effort. It requires consistent effort, providing value, and engaging with your subscribers on a regular basis. However, the rewards are well worth it. An email list is a powerful asset that can drive profitability and sustainability to your online business, regardless of your chosen niche.

In conclusion, if you want to make money online, building an email list and leveraging it for profit is a vital strategy. It allows you to establish a direct line of communication with your target audience, nurture relationships, and convert subscribers into paying customers. Regardless of your niche, incorporating email list building into your online business strategy will undoubtedly boost your profitability and help you achieve passive income mastery.

Chapter 4: E-commerce and Dropshipping

Understanding the E-commerce Business Model

In today's digital age, the e-commerce business model has become one of the most lucrative ways to make money online. Whether you're an aspiring entrepreneur or simply someone looking to earn some extra income, understanding how e-commerce works is vital. This subchapter will provide you with a comprehensive overview of the e-commerce business model, its benefits, and how you can get started.

E-commerce, or electronic commerce, refers to the buying and selling of goods and services over the internet. It has revolutionized the way people shop, allowing consumers to purchase products from the comfort of their homes. E-commerce offers numerous advantages over traditional brick-and- mortar stores, such as lower startup costs, wider customer reach, and the ability to operate 24/7.

To succeed in the e-commerce business, you need to choose a profitable niche that aligns with your interests and expertise. This book covers a wide range of niches, including make money with online passive income, blogging for profit, e-commerce and dropshipping, creating and selling digital products, social media management and marketing, podcasting, creating and selling online courses, freelancing, and online service-based businesses. Each niche has its own unique opportunities and challenges, so it's important to choose one that suits your skills and interests.

Once you've identified your niche, you can start building your e-commerce store. This can be done through popular platforms like Shopify, WooCommerce, or Etsy, depending on the type of products you plan to sell. It's crucial to create an attractive and user-friendly website that showcases your products and provides a seamless shopping experience for your customers.

In addition to setting up your online store, you'll also need to focus on driving traffic and generating sales. This can be achieved through various strategies, such as search engine optimization (SEO), social media marketing, influencer collaborations, email marketing, and paid advertising. It's essential to understand the basics of digital marketing to effectively promote your products and reach your target audience.

Furthermore, maintaining customer satisfaction and building a strong brand reputation are key factors in the long-term success of your e-commerce business. Providing excellent customer service, offering competitive prices, and delivering high-quality products are essential for building trust and loyalty with your customers.

In conclusion, understanding the e-commerce business model is crucial for anyone looking to make money online. By choosing a profitable niche, setting up an attractive online store, implementing effective marketing strategies, and prioritizing customer satisfaction, you can create a successful e- commerce business that generates passive income. This subchapter will provide you with the knowledge and tools to get started on your journey towards financial freedom.

Setting Up an Online Store with Shopify

In today's digital era, setting up an online store has become a popular way to generate passive income and make money online. One of the leading platforms for e-commerce is Shopify, which offers a user-friendly and comprehensive solution for entrepreneurs who want to start their online business.

Shopify provides a seamless experience for anyone looking to create an online store, regardless of their technical expertise. With its intuitive interface and customizable templates, you can easily set up a professional-looking online store that reflects your brand and attracts customers.

To begin setting up your online store with Shopify, the first step is to sign up for an account. Shopify offers different pricing plans, allowing you to choose the one that suits your needs and budget. Once you've signed up, you can start customizing your store by selecting a theme from the Shopify theme store or uploading your own design.

After selecting a theme, you can begin adding products to your store. Shopify provides a user-friendly interface for managing your inventory, including product descriptions, pricing, and images. You can also organize your products into different categories to make it easier for customers to navigate your store.

To ensure a seamless shopping experience for your customers, it's crucial to set up secure payment gateways. Shopify integrates with various payment providers, such as PayPal and Stripe, allowing you to accept credit card payments and other online payment methods. You can also offer different shipping options and set up automated shipping rates based on the customer's location.

Furthermore, Shopify offers numerous apps and integrations that can enhance your store's functionality. From email marketing tools to social media integrations, you can leverage these features to promote your products and reach a wider audience.

Once your store is set up, it's important to drive traffic and attract customers. This can be achieved through various marketing strategies, such as social media marketing, content marketing, and search engine optimization. Shopify provides built-in SEO tools to optimize your store for search engines, ensuring that your products appear in relevant search results.

Setting up an online store with Shopify is an excellent opportunity for anyone looking to make money online. Whether you're interested in e-commerce, dropshipping, or selling digital products, Shopify offers a comprehensive solution to help you launch and grow your online business. With its user- friendly interface, customizable themes, and extensive features, Shopify provides the tools you need to succeed in the world of online entrepreneurship.

Sourcing Products for Dropshipping

One of the most popular and lucrative methods of making money online is through dropshipping. This business model allows you to sell products without having to hold inventory or worry about shipping and fulfillment. In this subchapter, we will explore the best strategies for sourcing products for your dropshipping business.

When it comes to dropshipping, finding the right products is crucial for your success. You want to offer products that are in demand, have a good profit margin, and are easy to source.

Here are a few strategies you can use to source products for your dropshipping store:

1. Research popular niches: Start by researching popular niches in the market. Look for products that have a high demand and low competition. This will ensure that there is a ready market for your products and that you can stand out from your competitors.

2. Use dropshipping platforms: There are many dropshipping platforms available that can help you find products to sell. Platforms like AliExpress, Oberlo, and SaleHoo allow you to browse through thousands of products and connect with suppliers who are willing to dropship.

3. Attend trade shows and exhibitions: Trade shows and exhibitions are great places to find unique and innovative products. By attending these events, you can connect with manufacturers and suppliers directly, negotiate better deals, and discover new products before they hit the market.

4. Utilize social media and online communities: Social media platforms like Instagram, Facebook, and Pinterest are great places to discover trending products. Joining online communities and forums related to your niche can also provide valuable insights and recommendations for sourcing products.

5. Stay updated with industry trends: Keep an eye on the latest trends in your niche. Stay updated with industry news and follow influencers and thought leaders in your field. This will help you identify emerging trends and capitalize on them before your competitors.

Remember, when sourcing products for dropshipping, it's important to consider factors like product quality, shipping times, and customer reviews. Always test the products before adding them to your store and maintain open lines of communication with your suppliers to ensure a smooth and reliable supply chain.

In conclusion, sourcing products for dropshipping requires careful research, market analysis, and staying ahead of industry trends. By utilizing various strategies and platforms, you can find profitable products that resonate with your target audience and build a successful dropshipping business.

Marketing and Promoting Your E-commerce Store

In today's digital age, having an e-commerce store is one of the most lucrative ways to make money online. However, simply creating a store is not enough. To truly succeed, you need to effectively market and promote your e-commerce store to attract customers and increase sales. In this chapter, we will explore various strategies and techniques that will help you master the art of marketing and promoting your e-commerce store.

Social media is a powerful tool for reaching a wide audience and generating buzz for your e- commerce store. By creating engaging and shareable content, you can attract potential customers and drive traffic to your store. We will delve into the world of social media management and marketing, providing you with tips on how to effectively utilize platforms such as Facebook, Instagram, and Twitter to promote your store.

Another effective way to market your e-commerce store is through blogging. By creating valuable and informative content related to your niche, you can establish yourself as an authority and attract a loyal audience. We will explore the world of blogging for profit, offering insights on how to monetize your blog and drive traffic to your e-commerce store.

When it comes to e-commerce, one of the most popular business models is dropshipping. In this chapter, we will discuss strategies for effectively marketing and promoting your dropshipping store. From optimizing product listings to running targeted ads, we will cover everything you need to know to drive sales and maximize profits.

Additionally, we will explore the world of creating and selling digital products. Whether it's e-books, online courses, or software, digital products can be a fantastic source of passive income. We will provide you with tips on how to create and market these products, helping you generate a steady stream of income.

Lastly, we will delve into the world of podcasting and monetizing audio content. Podcasting has become increasingly popular in recent years, and it presents a unique opportunity to connect with your audience on a more personal level. We will discuss strategies for creating and promoting a successful podcast, as well as ways to monetize your audio content.

Whether you're running an e-commerce store, blogging for profit, or creating and selling digital products, mastering the art of marketing and promotion is essential for success. In this chapter, we will guide you through various strategies and techniques that will help you reach your target audience and achieve your financial goals. Get ready to take your e-commerce store to new heights!

Fulfillment and Customer Service Strategies

In today's digital world, where making money online has become a popular choice for many, it is crucial to understand the importance of fulfillment and customer service strategies. Whether you are involved in making money through online passive income, blogging for profit, e-commerce and dropshipping, creating and selling digital products, social media management and marketing, podcasting and monetizing audio content, creating and selling online courses, or freelancing and online service-based businesses, delivering exceptional customer service and ensuring efficient fulfillment are paramount to your success.

Fulfillment refers to the process of delivering the products or services to your customers. It involves inventory management, packaging, shipping, and handling returns. The key to successful fulfillment is to have a streamlined and efficient system in place. This includes partnering with reliable suppliers, automating processes, and utilizing technology to track orders and shipments. By optimizing your fulfillment process, you can ensure timely delivery, minimize errors, and enhance customer satisfaction.

Customer service, on the other hand, is the backbone of any business. It is about building strong relationships with your customers and providing them with personalized support. In the online world, where face-to-face interactions are limited, it becomes even more crucial to establish trust and engage with your customers. This can be achieved through various means such as prompt and helpful responses to inquiries, offering value-added services, and actively seeking feedback to continuously improve your offerings.

To excel in fulfillment and customer service, it is essential to prioritize your customers' needs and expectations. By understanding their pain points and desires, you can tailor your offerings and provide a seamless experience. Additionally, leveraging technology can help you automate certain aspects of customer service, such as chatbots for quick responses or CRM systems for managing customer interactions.

Remember, word-of-mouth is a powerful tool in the online world. Positive feedback and reviews from satisfied customers can significantly boost your reputation and attract more business. Conversely, negative experiences can harm your brand and hinder your growth. By focusing on fulfillment and customer service strategies, you can differentiate yourself from competitors, build a loyal customer base, and ultimately achieve long-term success in your online money-making endeavors.

In conclusion, regardless of the niche you are in, be it online passive income, blogging, e-commerce, digital products, social media marketing, podcasting, online courses, or freelancing, fulfillment and customer service are vital elements to master. By prioritizing the needs of your customers, streamlining your fulfillment process, and leveraging technology, you can create a positive and memorable experience that will drive customer loyalty and propel your business towards success.

Chapter 5: Creating and Selling Digital Products

Identifying Profitable Digital Product Ideas

In today's digital age, there are endless opportunities to make money online. Whether you're looking to start a side hustle or build a full-fledged online business, the key to success lies in identifying profitable digital product ideas. This subchapter will guide you through the process of finding lucrative niches and creating digital products that cater to the needs and desires of your target audience.

One of the first steps in identifying profitable digital product ideas is to understand the various niches within the online money-making world. There are several niches that have proven to be highly profitable, including make money with online passive income, blogging for profit, e-commerce and dropshipping, creating and selling digital products, social media management and marketing, podcasting and monetizing audio content, creating and selling online courses, and freelancing and online service-based businesses.

Once you have identified your niche, it's crucial to conduct thorough market research. This involves analyzing your target audience's pain points, desires, and purchasing behavior. By understanding their needs, you can create digital products that provide solutions and value.

To generate profitable digital product ideas, consider brainstorming sessions, competitor analysis, and customer surveys. Brainstorming sessions can help you generate unique and innovative ideas that haven't been explored yet. Competitor analysis allows you to identify gaps in the market and differentiate your products from existing ones. Customer surveys provide valuable insights into what your target audience is looking for, helping you tailor your offerings to their preferences.

When creating digital products, focus on delivering exceptional quality and value. Whether you're creating e-books, online courses, or digital templates, ensure that your products are informative, well- designed, and easy to use. This will not only attract customers but also build a loyal customer base that will eagerly recommend your products to others.

Lastly, don't forget the importance of marketing and promotion. Even the best digital products won't generate income if they aren't effectively marketed. Utilize social media platforms, content marketing strategies, email marketing campaigns, and collaborations with influencers to reach your target audience and drive sales.

In conclusion, identifying profitable digital product ideas is a crucial step in making money online. By understanding your niche, conducting market research, and creating high-quality products, you can build a successful online business and achieve financial freedom.

Creating High-Quality Digital Products

In today's digital age, creating high-quality digital products has become a lucrative avenue for making money online. Whether you are interested in blogging for profit, e-commerce and dropshipping, creating and selling digital products, social media management and marketing, podcasting and monetizing audio content, creating and selling online courses, or freelancing and online service-based businesses, this subchapter will provide you with valuable insights on how to create exceptional digital products that generate passive income.

When it comes to digital products, quality is paramount. The first step in creating high-quality digital products is to identify a niche that aligns with your interests and expertise. By choosing a niche you are passionate about, you can ensure that the content you produce is authentic and resonates with your target audience.

Once you have defined your niche, it is essential to conduct thorough market research. This involves analyzing your target audience's needs, preferences, and pain points. By understanding their desires and challenges, you can tailor your digital product to provide a solution that meets their specific requirements.

When creating your digital product, it is crucial to invest time and effort into developing compelling content. Whether it is an e-book, online course, or podcast series, ensure that your content is well- researched, organized, and presented professionally. Incorporate engaging visuals, interactive elements, and practical examples to enhance the overall user experience.

In addition to content, the design of your digital product plays a significant role in its quality. Utilize user-friendly platforms and tools to create visually appealing and intuitive interfaces. Pay attention to color schemes, typography, and overall aesthetics to create a visually cohesive and attractive product.

Testing and feedback are vital in the creation process. Before launching your digital product, conduct thorough testing to ensure that it functions flawlessly and provides a seamless user experience. Seek feedback from beta testers or early adopters to identify any areas for improvement and make necessary revisions.

Finally, marketing and promoting your digital product

effectively is crucial for generating passive income. Utilize various online platforms and social media channels to reach your target audience. Create compelling sales pages, utilize email marketing campaigns, and leverage influencer partnerships to increase visibility and drive sales.

In conclusion, creating high-quality digital products is a powerful way to generate passive income online. By identifying a niche, conducting market research, creating compelling content, focusing on design, testing thoroughly, and executing effective marketing strategies, you can create exceptional digital products that resonate with your target audience and generate a steady stream of income.

Establishing an Effective Sales Funnel

In today's digital age, the potential to make money online is vast and exciting. Whether you have a passion for blogging, e-commerce, podcasting, or creating and selling digital products, understanding how to establish an effective sales funnel is crucial for your success. A sales funnel is a strategic process that guides potential customers through a series of steps, ultimately leading to a purchase. It is the backbone of any online business and can significantly impact your passive income potential.

To establish an effective sales funnel, you must first understand your target audience. Who are they? What are their pain points and desires? By identifying your audience's needs, you can craft compelling messages that resonate with them. This requires thorough market research and an understanding of your niche.

Once you have a clear understanding of your target audience, it's time to create awareness and attract potential customers. This can be achieved through various marketing channels, such as social media, blogging, podcasting, or paid advertising. The key is to drive traffic to your website or landing page where you can capture their contact information.

Once you have captured their contact information, it's essential to nurture the relationship and build trust. This can be done through email marketing, providing valuable content, or offering freebies that address their pain points. The goal here is to position yourself as an expert in your niche and establish credibility.

As you continue to nurture the relationship, it's time to present your offer. This could be a digital product, an online course, or a service that solves your audience's problems. It's crucial to make the offer irresistible by highlighting its unique benefits and addressing any objections your audience may have.

Finally, it's time to seal the deal. This is where you convert your leads into paying customers. You can do this by creating a sense of urgency, offering limited-time discounts, or providing additional bonuses. It's important to make the buying process seamless and user-friendly to ensure a positive customer experience.

Remember, establishing an effective sales funnel takes time and experimentation. It's essential to track your metrics, analyze your results, and make necessary adjustments along the way. By continuously optimizing your funnel, you can maximize your passive income potential and achieve long-term success in your chosen niche.

In conclusion, whether you're interested in blogging, e-commerce, podcasting, or creating online courses, understanding how to establish an effective sales funnel is essential. It allows you to attract, nurture, and convert potential customers into paying ones. By following the steps outlined in this subchapter, you can significantly enhance your passive income potential and achieve your financial goals.

Launching and Marketing Your Digital Products

Launching and marketing your digital products is a crucial step in building a successful online business and achieving passive income. Whether you are a blogger, e-commerce entrepreneur, course creator, or freelancer, effectively promoting your products is essential to attract customers and generate revenue. In this subchapter, we will explore various strategies and techniques to help you master the art of launching and marketing your digital products.

First and foremost, it is important to understand your target audience and their needs. By identifying your niche and understanding the problems your audience is facing, you can develop digital products that provide valuable solutions. Conduct thorough market research and use customer feedback to refine your offerings.

Once your digital products are ready, it's time to create a launch plan. Begin by building anticipation and excitement around your products. Utilize social media platforms, email marketing, and your blog to create buzz. Consider offering exclusive discounts or bonuses to early adopters to encourage sales.

Next, leverage the power of social media to reach a wider audience. Develop a solid social media strategy and consistently engage with your followers. Share valuable content, sneak peeks of your products, and customer testimonials to build credibility and trust. Collaborate with influencers in your niche to expand your reach and gain exposure to new potential customers.

In addition to social media, consider starting a podcast or producing audio content to promote your digital products. Podcasting has become increasingly popular and provides a unique opportunity to connect with your audience on a more personal level. Monetize your audio content by incorporating product promotions and sponsorships.

Creating and selling online courses is another lucrative avenue to explore. Develop comprehensive and high-quality courses that cater to the needs of your target audience. Use platforms like Udemy or Teachable to host and sell your courses. Implement effective marketing techniques such as offering free previews, testimonials, and limited-time discounts to entice potential students.

Lastly, consider partnering with other businesses or influencers to cross-promote your digital products. Collaborations can help you tap into new customer bases and increase brand visibility. Additionally, explore different advertising channels such as Google AdWords or Facebook Ads to reach potential customers who may not be familiar with your brand.

Launching and marketing your digital products requires careful planning, strategic thinking, and consistent effort. By understanding your target audience, utilizing social media, creating engaging content, and exploring various promotional avenues, you can successfully generate passive income and build a thriving online business.

Optimizing Your Sales and Scaling Your Business

In the ever-evolving digital landscape, the opportunities for making money online are endless. Whether you're looking to generate passive income or launch your own online business, this subchapter has got you covered. We will explore various strategies to optimize your sales and scale your business to new heights, catering to a wide range of niches including online passive income, blogging for profit, e-commerce and dropshipping, creating and selling digital products, social media management and marketing, podcasting and monetizing audio content, creating and selling online courses, freelancing, and online service-based businesses.

Firstly, we will delve into the world of online passive income. From affiliate marketing to digital real estate, we will guide you through the process of setting up multiple income streams that can generate revenue while you sleep. We will explore the importance of choosing the right niche, building a solid online presence, and utilizing effective marketing strategies to boost your sales.

Next, we will explore the art of blogging for profit. We will provide you with insider tips on creating engaging and valuable content, increasing your website traffic, and monetizing your blog through various revenue streams such as sponsored posts, advertisements, and affiliate marketing.

If e-commerce and dropshipping are your passions, we will take you through the steps of starting your own online store, selecting the right products, and implementing effective marketing strategies to maximize your sales. We will share industry insights and best practices to help you thrive in the competitive online marketplace.

For those interested in creating and selling digital products, we will guide you through the process of product development, pricing, and marketing. Whether it's e-books, online courses, or software, we will equip you with the knowledge and tools to turn your expertise into profitable digital products.

Social media management and marketing have become indispensable tools for businesses of all sizes. We will provide you with strategies to build a strong social media presence, engage with your audience, and convert followers into paying customers.

Moreover, we will explore the world of podcasting and guide you on how to create engaging audio content, build a loyal listener base, and monetize your podcast through sponsorships, advertising, and merchandise sales.

Online courses have gained immense popularity, and we will show you how to create and sell your own. From topic selection and course structure to marketing and pricing, we will help you create a successful online learning platform.

Lastly, for those interested in freelancing and online service-based businesses, we will provide guidance on building a strong portfolio, effectively marketing your services, and scaling your business by attracting high-paying clients.

No matter your niche or area of interest, this subchapter will equip you with the essential strategies to optimize your sales and scale your online business. Get ready to take your entrepreneurial journey to new heights and start making money online today!

Chapter 6: Social Media Management and Marketing

Understanding the Power of Social Media for Business

Social media has become an integral part of our everyday lives, and its impact on businesses cannot be denied. Whether you are starting an online passive income business, blogging for profit, managing an e-commerce store, creating digital products, or running any other online venture, understanding the power of social media is crucial for your success.

One of the primary reasons why social media holds such power for businesses is its ability to reach a massive audience. Platforms like Facebook, Instagram, Twitter, and LinkedIn have billions of active users, providing an unprecedented opportunity to connect with potential customers. By strategically leveraging social media, you can increase brand visibility, attract new customers, and ultimately boost your sales.

Furthermore, social media platforms also offer advanced targeting and advertising options. This means you can reach a specific audience based on demographics, interests, and behaviors, ensuring that your marketing efforts are reaching the right people. Unlike traditional advertising methods, social media ads are cost-effective and can be customized to fit your budget.

Another benefit of social media for business is the ability to build and nurture relationships with your audience. By engaging with your followers through comments, direct messages, and sharing valuable content, you can establish trust and loyalty. This, in turn, leads to increased customer retention and word-of-mouth referrals.

Moreover, social media provides an excellent platform for showcasing your expertise and building your personal brand. By consistently sharing valuable content related to your niche, you can position yourself as an authority in your industry. This not only helps attract potential customers but also opens up opportunities for partnerships, collaborations, and speaking engagements.

In addition to these benefits, social media also plays a significant role in customer service. Customers now expect businesses to be responsive and available on social media platforms. By promptly addressing their queries, concerns, and complaints, you can enhance customer satisfaction and improve your brand's reputation.

To fully harness the power of social media, it is essential to develop a comprehensive social media strategy tailored to your business goals and target audience. This includes identifying the most relevant platforms for your niche, creating engaging and shareable content, and tracking the effectiveness of your campaigns through analytics.

In conclusion, social media has revolutionized the way businesses operate. It has the power to reach and engage a massive audience, boost brand visibility, drive sales, and build meaningful relationships with customers. By understanding and leveraging the potential of social media, you can take your online business to new heights of success.

Creating a Social Media Strategy for Your Business

In today's digital age, having a strong social media presence is crucial for any business looking to make money online. With millions of potential customers scrolling through various platforms every day, it's essential to have a well-thought-out social media strategy in place. This subchapter will guide you through the process of creating an effective social media strategy that aligns with your business goals.

1. Define your objectives:
Before diving into the world of social media, it's important to identify your business objectives. Whether it's increasing brand awareness, driving traffic to your website, or boosting sales, having clear goals will help you tailor your social media strategy accordingly.

2. Know your target audience:
Understanding your target audience is key to creating engaging content that resonates with them. Take the time to research and analyze your audience's demographics, interests, and online behavior. This information will enable you to choose the right social media platforms and craft content that appeals to your audience.

3. Choose the right platforms:
Not all social media platforms are created equal. Each platform has its own unique features and user base. Based on your target audience's preferences, select the platforms that align with your business goals. For example, if you're targeting a younger demographic, platforms like Instagram and TikTok might be more suitable, whereas LinkedIn may be ideal for targeting professionals.

4. Develop a content strategy:
Creating engaging and valuable content is the heart of any successful social media strategy. Determine the types of content that resonate with your audience, whether it's blog

posts, videos, infographics, or podcasts. Plan a content calendar to ensure consistency and variety.

5. Engage with your audience:
Social media is all about building relationships and engaging with your audience. Respond to comments, messages, and reviews promptly. Encourage user-generated content and run contests or giveaways to foster a sense of community.

6. Measure and analyze:
Regularly track your social media metrics to gauge the effectiveness of your strategy. Analyze data such as reach, engagement, click-through rates, and conversions. This information will help you identify what's working and what needs improvement, allowing you to refine your strategy for better results.

Remember, social media is not just a platform to showcase your products or services. It's about building connections, providing value, and creating a community around your brand. By implementing an effective social media strategy, you can leverage these platforms to grow your online passive income, boost blog profitability, drive sales in e-commerce and dropshipping, sell digital products, manage social media marketing, monetize audio content through podcasting, create and sell online courses, and succeed in freelancing and online service-based businesses.

Building and Engaging Your Social Media Audience

In today's digital era, social media has become an indispensable tool for individuals and businesses alike. It has revolutionized the way we connect, communicate, and consume information. For aspiring entrepreneurs and those seeking to make money online, harnessing the power of social media is crucial in building a successful online presence and generating passive income.

Whether your niche is blogging for profit, e-commerce, creating digital products, social media management, podcasting, online courses, or freelancing, understanding how to build and engage your social media audience is paramount.

The first step in building your social media audience is to identify your target market. Who are your potential customers? What are their interests, pain points, and preferences? By understanding your audience, you can create content that resonates with them and grabs their attention.

Once you know your target market, it's time to select the right social media platforms. Each platform has its own unique audience and features, so it's essential to choose the ones that align with your niche and target market. Whether it's

Facebook, Instagram, Twitter, LinkedIn, or YouTube, focus on platforms where your audience spends the most time.

Creating compelling content is the key to engaging your social media audience. Share valuable insights, tips, and solutions to their problems. Use eye-catching visuals, videos, and infographics to capture their attention. Encourage interaction by asking questions, running polls, and responding to comments. Remember, social media is a two-way street, so make sure to engage with your audience by liking, commenting, and sharing their posts.

Consistency is vital in building and engaging your social media audience. Develop a content calendar and stick to a regular posting schedule. Provide fresh and relevant content consistently to keep your audience interested and coming back for more. Utilize social media management tools to schedule posts in advance, ensuring a consistent flow of content even during busy periods.

Lastly, leverage the power of analytics to track your social media performance. Monitor your engagement metrics, such as likes, comments, shares, and click-through rates. Analyze which types of content resonate the most with your audience and adjust your strategy accordingly. Continuously refine your approach based on data-driven insights to optimize your social media presence and grow your audience.

Building and engaging your social media audience is a continuous process. It requires time, effort, and a deep understanding of your target market. By consistently delivering valuable content, engaging with your audience, and leveraging analytics, you can build a loyal following, drive traffic to your online ventures, and ultimately achieve your goal of making money online.

Leveraging Social Media Advertising for Greater Reach

In today's digital age, social media platforms have become powerful tools for businesses and individuals alike. With millions of users actively engaging on platforms such as Facebook, Instagram, Twitter, and LinkedIn, it's no wonder why savvy entrepreneurs are turning to social media advertising to reach a wider audience and maximize their profits. In this subchapter, we will explore how you can leverage social media advertising to generate passive income and boost your online presence.

One of the most significant advantages of social media advertising is its ability to target specific demographics. Whether you're in the niche of making money with online passive income, blogging for profit, e-commerce and dropshipping, creating and selling digital products, social media management and marketing, podcasting and monetizing audio content, creating and selling online courses, or freelancing and online service-based businesses, social media platforms allow you to precisely target your desired audience. By utilizing the advanced targeting options available, you can ensure that your ads are seen by the right people at the right time, increasing your chances of conversion.

Additionally, social media advertising offers various ad formats to suit your marketing objectives. From image-based ads to video ads and carousel ads, you can choose the format that best showcases your products or services and captures the attention of your target audience. This versatility allows you to experiment with different ad formats to determine which ones generate the highest engagement and conversions.

Furthermore, social media advertising provides valuable analytics and insights that enable you to measure the performance of your ads. By tracking metrics such as impressions, click-through rates, and conversions, you can gain valuable insights into the effectiveness of your campaigns. Armed with this data, you can make data-driven decisions to optimize your ads and improve your return on investment.

To effectively leverage social media advertising for greater reach, it's essential to develop a comprehensive strategy. Begin by identifying your target audience and understanding their interests, behaviors, and pain points. Then, create compelling ad copy and visuals that resonate with your audience and compel them to take action. Monitor the performance of your ads regularly and make adjustments as necessary to maximize your results.

By harnessing the power of social media advertising, you can expand your reach, attract more customers, and ultimately increase your passive income. With careful planning and execution, social media advertising can become an invaluable tool in your journey towards financial success in the online world.

Measuring and Analyzing Your Social Media ROI

In today's digital world, social media has become an indispensable tool for individuals and businesses alike. Not only does it allow us to connect with friends and family, but it also provides endless opportunities to make money online. However, to succeed in the vast landscape of social media, it is crucial to measure and analyze your social media return on investment (ROI).

For people looking to make money online in various niches such as blogging for profit, e-commerce and dropshipping, creating and selling digital products, social media management and marketing, podcasting and monetizing audio content, creating and selling online courses, freelancing, and online service-based businesses, understanding and optimizing your social media ROI is paramount.

Measuring and analyzing your social media ROI involves tracking and evaluating the effectiveness of your social media efforts in generating revenue and achieving business goals. It allows you to gain valuable insights into the performance of your social media campaigns, identify what is working and what isn't, and make data-driven decisions to improve your strategies.

There are several key metrics and tools you can use to measure and analyze your social media ROI effectively. For example, tracking the number of followers, likes, shares, comments, and engagement rates can give you an idea of your social media reach and impact. Additionally, monitoring website traffic, conversions, and revenue generated from social media referrals can help you determine the monetary value of your social media efforts.

To accurately measure and analyze your social media ROI, it is crucial to set clear and measurable goals that align with your overall business objectives. Whether it's increasing sales, driving traffic to your website, or boosting brand awareness, defining specific goals will allow you to track progress and assess the success of your social media campaigns.

Furthermore, utilizing social media analytics tools such as Google Analytics, Facebook Insights, or Instagram Insights can provide you with in-depth data and reports on your social media performance. These tools can help you identify trends, demographics, and user behavior, enabling you to fine-tune your strategies and target the right audience effectively.

By measuring and analyzing your social media ROI, you can optimize your efforts, allocate resources wisely, and maximize your returns. It allows you to identify the most effective social media platforms, content types, and strategies for your specific niche and target audience. Ultimately, this knowledge will help you make informed decisions, refine your approach, and achieve your goals of making money online through various passive income streams.

Chapter 7: Podcasting and Monetizing Audio Content

The Rise of Podcasting as a Profitable Medium

In recent years, podcasting has emerged as an incredibly lucrative medium for individuals looking to make money online. With its low barriers to entry, wide reach, and growing popularity, podcasting offers numerous opportunities for those seeking to generate passive income and build a successful online business.

One of the main reasons podcasting has become such a profitable medium is its ability to reach a global audience. Unlike traditional radio shows or TV programs, podcasts can be accessed anytime, anywhere, and on any device. This accessibility has allowed podcasters to connect with millions of listeners worldwide, creating a vast potential for monetization.

For those looking to make money with online passive income, podcasting offers various revenue streams. Advertisements and sponsorships are common ways for podcasters to generate income. As your podcast grows in popularity, you can partner with brands and companies that align with your niche to promote their products or services. These collaborations can be highly lucrative, especially if you have a dedicated and engaged audience.

Furthermore, podcasting can be a powerful tool for bloggers looking to monetize their content. By repurposing their blog posts into podcast episodes or creating exclusive audio content, bloggers can expand their reach and attract new audiences. This, in turn, can lead to increased traffic to their blogs and opportunities for affiliate marketing or selling digital products.

E-commerce and dropshipping entrepreneurs can also benefit from podcasting. By leveraging the power of audio storytelling, podcasters can build trust and credibility with their listeners, making it easier to promote and sell products they have sourced or created. Additionally, podcasting allows for the creation of a strong community around your brand, fostering customer loyalty and repeat business.

Creating and selling digital products is another niche that can be highly profitable through podcasting. As a podcaster, you can offer exclusive bonus content, courses, or e-books to your listeners, providing them with valuable resources while generating revenue for yourself. By leveraging your expertise and building a loyal audience, you can establish yourself as an authority in your field and attract paying customers.

Social media management and marketing professionals can also find podcasting to be a valuable addition to their services. By creating engaging and informative podcast episodes, you can showcase your expertise, attract new clients, and even offer premium consulting services to businesses looking to leverage the power of podcasting for their marketing efforts.

In summary, the rise of podcasting as a profitable medium offers a plethora of opportunities for individuals across various niches to make money online. Whether you are interested in online passive income, blogging for profit, e-commerce and dropshipping, creating and selling digital products, social media management and marketing, podcasting and monetizing audio content, creating and selling online courses, or freelancing and online service-based businesses, podcasting can be a game-changer for your online income generation. With its global reach, diverse revenue streams, and potential for building a loyal audience, podcasting should not be overlooked as a profitable medium in the ever-expanding world of online business.

Planning and Launching Your Podcast

Podcasting has become an increasingly popular way to make money online, and with good reason. It allows you to reach a wide audience, establish yourself as an expert in your niche, and generate passive income through sponsorships, advertising, and product sales. If you're interested in diving into the world of podcasting, this subchapter will guide you through the planning and launching process.

1. Define Your Niche: The first step in planning your podcast is to identify your target audience and determine the niche you want to focus on. Consider your expertise, interests, and the needs of your potential listeners. Are you passionate about online passive income, blogging for profit, e-commerce and dropshipping, creating and selling digital products, social media management and marketing, podcasting and monetizing audio content, creating and selling online courses, or freelancing and online service-based businesses?

2. Set Clear Goals: Determine what you want to achieve with your podcast. Is it to educate, entertain, or inspire your audience? Are you looking to generate income directly from the podcast or use it as a marketing tool for your other online ventures? Clearly define your goals to guide your content creation and monetization strategies.

3. Plan Your Content: Brainstorm ideas for podcast episodes that align with your niche and target audience. Create an editorial calendar to ensure consistent and engaging content. Consider interviewing experts in your field, sharing valuable tips and insights, and addressing common challenges faced by your audience.

4. Choose Your Format and Equipment: Decide whether you want to host a solo show, co-host with someone else, or have guest interviews. Research and invest in quality podcasting equipment including a microphone, headphones, and recording software to ensure professional audio quality.

5. Create Engaging Cover Art and Intro Music: Your podcast cover art and intro music are crucial for attracting new listeners. Hire a graphic designer to create eye-catching cover art that reflects your podcast's theme, and consider licensing or creating original intro music that captures the essence of your show.

6. Set Up Hosting and Distribution: Choose a reliable podcast hosting platform that provides analytics, easy distribution to major podcast directories, and monetization options. Some popular hosting platforms include Libsyn, Podbean, and Buzzsprout.

7. Launch and Promote: Once your podcast is set up, launch it with a captivating episode. Promote your podcast through your existing online channels, such as your blog, social media accounts, and email list. Consider collaborating with other podcasters or influencers in your niche to expand your reach.

Remember, podcasting is not an overnight success. It

requires consistent effort, high-quality content, and effective marketing strategies. However, if you plan and launch your podcast with a clear vision and dedication, it can become a profitable source of passive income and a valuable asset for your online business.

Creating Engaging and Valuable Podcast Content

In today's digital age, podcasting has become an increasingly popular medium for sharing information and connecting with an audience. With millions of podcast episodes available at the touch of a button, it's crucial to create content that stands out from the crowd. Whether you're a seasoned podcast host or just getting started, this subchapter will guide you on how to create engaging and valuable podcast content that attracts listeners and generates passive income.

Firstly, it's important to identify your target audience and niche. Understanding who you are speaking to will help you tailor your content to their interests and needs. Choose a topic within the niches of Make Money with Online Passive Income, Blogging for profit, E-commerce and dropshipping, Creating and selling digital products, Social media management and marketing, Podcasting and monetizing audio content, Creating and selling online courses, or Freelancing and online service-based businesses. This will ensure that your podcast content is relevant and resonates with your listeners.

Next, focus on creating high-quality and engaging episodes. Research and prepare your topics thoroughly, ensuring that they provide value and solve problems for your audience. Incorporate storytelling techniques, interviews with industry experts, and practical tips to keep your listeners engaged and coming back for more. Remember, your podcast content should be informative, entertaining, and actionable.

Additionally, consider the format and length of your episodes. While some podcasts thrive on longer, in-depth conversations, others may benefit from shorter, more concise episodes. Experiment with different lengths and formats to find what works best for your audience. Remember to keep your episodes focused and well-structured, ensuring that each episode has a clear purpose and takeaway.

Furthermore, leverage the power of promotion to reach a wider audience. Utilize social media platforms, email marketing, and collaborations with other podcasters to spread the word about your episodes. Engage with your listeners by encouraging feedback, questions, and suggestions. Building a community around your podcast will not only increase your reach but also provide valuable insights for improving your content.

Lastly, monetize your podcast through various income streams. Explore options such as sponsorships, affiliate marketing, premium content, merchandise, and crowdfunding. Choose revenue streams that align with your niche and add value to your listeners' experience. Remember, providing valuable content consistently is key to building a loyal audience who will support your podcast financially.

In conclusion, creating engaging and valuable podcast content is a vital component of building a successful online business. By identifying your target audience, delivering high-quality episodes, promoting your podcast effectively, and monetizing your content strategically, you can turn your passion for podcasting into a profitable venture. So, get behind the mic, share your knowledge, and start generating passive income through captivating podcast content.

Monetizing Your Podcast through Sponsorships and Ads

Podcasting has emerged as a popular and effective medium for sharing knowledge, stories, and entertainment. With the rise of digital media, podcasts have become a valuable tool not only for content creators but also for those seeking to make money online. One lucrative avenue for monetizing your podcast is through sponsorships and advertisements. In this chapter, we will explore the strategies and best practices to help you maximize your podcast's earning potential.

Sponsorships are a common way to monetize podcasts. As your podcast gains popularity and a dedicated audience, businesses and brands may be interested in sponsoring your show. These sponsors can provide financial support in exchange for exposure to your listeners. When seeking sponsorship opportunities, it's important to align with brands that resonate with your podcast's niche and audience. This ensures a natural fit and enhances the value for both you and the sponsor.

To attract sponsors, focus on building a strong brand and audience engagement. Consistently deliver high-quality content that resonates with your listeners. Engage with your audience through social media, email newsletters, and other platforms to build a loyal community. Sponsors will be more inclined to partner with you if they see a dedicated and engaged audience.

In addition to sponsorships, advertisements can be a profitable way to monetize your podcast. Platforms like Google AdSense and podcast-specific ad networks offer opportunities to display targeted ads within your episodes. These ads generate revenue based on impressions or clicks. However, it's essential to strike a balance between ads and content to maintain listener engagement. Too many ads can be off-putting, so carefully select the number and placement of ads to ensure a seamless listening experience.

When incorporating ads, transparency is key. Clearly indicate when an ad is being presented to your audience to maintain trust and authenticity. Consider creating custom ad spots that are integrated into your content, rather than simply reading a script. This personalized approach helps to create a seamless transition from content to advertisement, keeping your listeners engaged.

Remember, building a successful podcast takes time and effort. It's crucial to consistently provide value to your audience and adapt to their needs. By monetizing your podcast through sponsorships and ads, you can turn your passion into a profitable venture. Explore different avenues, experiment with different strategies, and always prioritize the needs and interests of your audience. With dedication and perseverance, you can unlock the potential of your podcast as a lucrative online business.

Growing Your Podcast Audience and Maximizing Revenue

In today's digital age, podcasting has become one of the most popular mediums for content consumption and entertainment. With millions of active listeners around the world, podcasting presents a unique opportunity for individuals to not only share their ideas and passions but also generate a substantial income stream. In this subchapter, we will explore proven strategies for growing your podcast audience and maximizing revenue.

1. Engaging Content: The key to attracting and retaining listeners is to produce high-quality, engaging content. Identify your target audience and create episodes that cater to their interests and needs. Conduct interviews with industry experts, share valuable insights, and provide actionable takeaways in each episode.

2. Consistent Release Schedule: Consistency is crucial in building a loyal audience. Develop a predictable release schedule, whether it's weekly, bi-weekly, or monthly, and stick to it. Regularly delivering new episodes will keep your audience engaged and eagerly awaiting your next release.

3. Optimize for Search Engines: Just like with blogging, optimizing your podcast for search engines can significantly boost your visibility. Use relevant keywords in your episode titles, descriptions, and show notes. This will help potential listeners discover your podcast when they search for related topics.

4. Leverage Social Media: Social media platforms are powerful tools for promoting your podcast. Create dedicated pages and profiles for your show on platforms like Facebook, Instagram, and Twitter. Share snippets of your episodes, engage with your audience, and encourage them to share your content with their networks.

5. Collaborate and Cross-Promote: Partnering with other podcasters in your niche can expand your reach and attract new listeners. Guest appearances on other shows or hosting guest episodes on your podcast can introduce your content to a wider audience. Additionally, consider cross-promoting each other's shows through shout-outs or promotional spots.

6. Monetizing Your Podcast: There are several ways to monetize your podcast and turn it into a revenue-generating asset. Explore sponsorship opportunities by reaching out to relevant companies in your niche. Offer premium content or bonus episodes through a subscription model. Create merchandise or courses related to your podcast's theme. You can also leverage affiliate marketing by promoting products or services that align with your audience's interests.

7. Engage with Your Audience: Building a relationship with your listeners is essential for long-term success. Encourage feedback, questions, and suggestions from your audience. Respond to comments and messages promptly, and consider hosting live Q&A sessions or

meetups to connect with your fans directly.

In conclusion, growing your podcast audience and maximizing revenue requires a combination of creating compelling content, optimizing for search engines, leveraging social media, collaborating with others, and exploring various monetization strategies. By implementing these strategies and staying committed to consistently delivering value to your audience, you can turn your podcast into a profitable venture while sharing your passion with the world.

Chapter 8: Creating and Selling Online Courses

Identifying Your Expertise and Course Topic

In today's digital age, making money online has become a sought-after goal for many individuals. With the rise of various online platforms and opportunities, it has never been easier to turn your passion and expertise into a lucrative source of income. If you are someone who wants to make money online, whether through passive income streams or active ventures, it is crucial to identify your expertise and course topic to maximize your potential for success.

One of the first steps in creating a profitable online business is to determine your niche or area of expertise. This is essential as it allows you to position yourself as an authority in your chosen field, making it easier to attract and engage with your target audience. By understanding your skills, knowledge, and interests, you can identify the areas where you excel and have a competitive advantage.

For those looking to make money with online passive income, it is essential to assess your strengths and interests in various niches. Whether it's blogging for profit, e-commerce and dropshipping, creating and selling digital products, or social media management and marketing, identifying your expertise in these areas will help you narrow down your focus and build a successful online business.

If you are passionate about writing and have a way with words, blogging for profit might be the perfect avenue for you. By choosing a niche that aligns with your interests and expertise, you can create engaging and valuable content that attracts a loyal audience and monetize your blog through various income streams, such as affiliate marketing and sponsored content.

Alternatively, if you have a flair for creativity and enjoy designing and selling products, e-commerce and dropshipping might be your calling. By identifying your expertise in this area, you can source and sell products that resonate with your target audience, leveraging platforms like Shopify and Amazon to generate passive income.

Creating and selling digital products, such as e-books, online courses, or templates, is another lucrative option for those with specialized knowledge or skills. By identifying your expertise in a specific field, you can create valuable digital products that solve your audience's pain points and generate passive income.

Social media management and marketing have become essential for businesses in the online world. If you have a deep understanding of social media platforms and strategies, you can offer your expertise as a social media manager or consultant, helping businesses grow their online presence and generating income through your services.

Other potential avenues for making money online include podcasting and monetizing audio content, creating and selling online courses, and freelancing in various service-based businesses. By identifying your expertise in these areas, you can leverage your skills and knowledge to create valuable content, products, or services that resonate with your target audience.

In conclusion, finding your expertise and course topic is crucial for anyone looking to make money online. By identifying your strengths, interests, and areas of expertise, you can position yourself as an authority in your niche and create valuable content, products, or services that attract and engage your target audience. Whether you choose to pursue passive income streams or active ventures, understanding your expertise is the first step towards achieving financial success in the online world.

Planning and Structuring Your Online Course

In today's digital age, making money online has become a popular avenue for individuals wanting to take control of their financial future. Whether you're interested in creating a passive income stream or starting a profitable online business, one of the most effective ways to achieve your goals is through creating and selling online courses. This subchapter will guide you through the process of planning and structuring your online course to maximize its impact and profitability.

Before diving into the planning phase, it's crucial to identify your target audience and niche. Understanding the specific needs and desires of your audience will enable you to create a course that resonates with them and provides value. Whether your niche is making money with online passive income, blogging for profit, e-commerce and dropshipping, creating and selling digital products, social media management and marketing, podcasting and monetizing audio content, or freelancing and online service-based businesses, tailoring your course content to address their pain points will increase its marketability.

Once you've defined your target audience and niche, it's time to outline your course content. Start by breaking down your course into modules or lessons, ensuring a logical flow of information. Each module should have a clear objective and focus on a specific topic, allowing your students to progress smoothly through the material. Consider using a mix of text, images, videos, and interactive elements to keep your course engaging and accessible.

To enhance the learning experience, incorporate assessments and assignments throughout the course. This will not only help students retain the information but also provide them with a sense of accomplishment and progress. Additionally, consider including a discussion forum or a community aspect to foster interaction and collaboration among your students.

Launching your online course requires careful planning and execution. Determine the best platform to host your course, ensuring it has the necessary features and capabilities to deliver your content effectively. Develop a marketing strategy that encompasses social media promotion, email marketing, and collaborations with influencers in your niche to generate buzz and attract potential students. Don't forget to set a competitive pricing strategy that reflects the value you're providing while remaining appealing to your target audience.

By planning and structuring your online course with your

audience in mind, you can create a profitable and impactful learning experience. With determination, dedication, and the right strategies, you'll be well on your way to achieving your financial goals through online course creation.

Creating Engaging and High-Quality Course Content

In today's digital age, online courses have become a popular way to make money and share knowledge with a global audience. However, with the increasing number of online courses available, it is crucial to create engaging and high-quality content that stands out from the competition. This subchapter will provide you with valuable insights and strategies to create compelling course content that resonates with your audience and helps you establish yourself as an authority in your niche.

When creating course content, it is essential to start by identifying your target audience and understanding their needs and pain points. What are the problems they are facing? How can your course provide them with a solution? By addressing these questions, you can tailor your content to meet the specific needs of your audience, making it more relevant and engaging.

One key aspect of creating high-quality course content is to ensure that it is well-structured and organized. Break down the course into modules and lessons, and provide a clear roadmap for your students to follow. This will help them navigate through the material easily and stay engaged throughout the course.

To make your course content more engaging, consider incorporating different types of media, such as videos, audios, quizzes, and interactive elements. Visuals and multimedia can enhance the learning experience and make the content more memorable for your students.

Another important element to consider is the use of storytelling. People connect with stories, so try to incorporate real-life examples, case studies, and personal anecdotes that illustrate the concepts you are teaching. This will make the content more relatable and help your students understand how to apply the knowledge in real-world situations.

Furthermore, encourage active participation from your students by including interactive elements in your course content. This could include assignments, discussion forums, or live Q&A sessions. By creating opportunities for students to engage with the material and each other, you foster a sense of community and increase the value they derive from the course.

Lastly, regularly update and improve your course content

based on feedback from your students. Pay attention to their comments, questions, and suggestions, and use this information to refine and enhance your content. By continuously improving your course, you not only provide a better learning experience for your students but also position yourself as an expert in your niche.

Creating engaging and high-quality course content is crucial to your success in the online education industry. By following the strategies outlined in this subchapter, you can create courses that not only generate passive income but also provide real value to your students. Remember to stay focused on your audience's needs and continuously strive for improvement to stay ahead in this competitive market.

Launching and Marketing Your Online Course

In today's digital age, creating and selling online courses has become a popular way to generate passive income. With the advancements in technology and the increasing demand for knowledge and skills, there has never been a better time to launch your own online course. In this subchapter, we will explore the strategies and techniques you can use to successfully launch and market your online course.

Before diving into the marketing aspect, it is crucial to ensure that your online course is well-crafted and valuable. Take the time to research your target audience's needs and preferences, and develop a course that addresses those pain points. Quality content is the foundation of any successful online course, so invest time and effort into creating engaging and informative modules.

Once your course is ready, it's time to launch and market it to your target audience. One effective strategy is to leverage your existing online presence. If you have a blog, e-commerce store, or social media following, promote your online course to your existing audience. Tailor your messaging to highlight the benefits and value your course offers.

In addition to leveraging your existing audience, consider collaborating with influencers or industry experts in your niche. Reach out to relevant influencers and offer them a free access pass to your course in exchange for a review or promotion. This can help you tap into their existing audience and increase your course's exposure.

Another effective marketing tactic is to utilize social media platforms. Create engaging and informative content related to your course topic to attract and engage your target audience. Use relevant hashtags, join relevant groups and communities, and interact with your audience to build credibility and trust.

Email marketing is another powerful tool in your marketing arsenal. Create a compelling lead magnet, such as an ebook or a mini-course, to entice potential customers to join your email list. Once they are on your list, nurture them with valuable content and occasionally promote your online course.

Lastly, consider hosting webinars or live Q&A sessions to generate excitement and interest in your course. Provide a sneak peek into your course content and answer any questions your audience may have. This interactive approach can help build trust and encourage conversions.

Launching and marketing your online course requires careful planning and execution. By leveraging your existing online presence, collaborating with influencers, utilizing social media, email marketing, and hosting webinars, you can effectively reach and convert your target audience. Remember, success in selling online courses lies in delivering value and building relationships with your audience.

Providing Ongoing Support and Maximizing Course Sales

In today's digital age, creating and selling online courses has become an increasingly popular way to make money online. Whether you are a subject matter expert or an experienced professional in your field, online courses offer a lucrative opportunity to share your knowledge and monetize your expertise. However, simply creating and launching a course is not enough. To maximize your course sales and provide ongoing support to your students, you need to employ effective strategies. This subchapter explores the key elements of providing ongoing support and maximizing course sales.

One of the most important aspects of maximizing course sales is to create a compelling sales page. Your sales page should clearly communicate the benefits of your course, highlight the value it offers, and provide social proof through testimonials and success stories. It should also include a call-to- action that encourages potential students to enroll in your course.

Once you have successfully sold your course, it is crucial to provide ongoing support to your students. This can be done through various means such as a private Facebook group, a dedicated forum, or regular Q&A sessions. By creating a community around your course, you not only provide additional value to your students but also foster a sense of belonging and accountability.

Another effective strategy to maximize course sales is to offer upsells and cross-sells. Upsells involve offering additional, more advanced content or services to students who have already enrolled in your course. Cross-sells, on the other hand, involve promoting related products or courses to your existing students. By leveraging the trust and relationship you have built with your students, these strategies can significantly increase your revenue and customer lifetime value.

Additionally, leveraging social media and email marketing can help you reach a wider audience and promote your course effectively. By creating engaging content, sharing success stories, and offering exclusive discounts or bonuses, you can attract potential students and encourage them to enroll in your course.

Lastly, continuously improving and updating your course content is essential to ensure its relevance and value. By collecting feedback from your students, monitoring industry trends, and staying up-to- date with the latest developments in your field, you can consistently enhance your course and provide an exceptional learning experience.

In conclusion, providing ongoing support and maximizing course sales is crucial for anyone looking to make money online through creating and selling online courses. By employing effective marketing strategies, offering ongoing support, and continuously improving your course content, you can not only increase your course sales but also establish yourself as an authority in your niche. So, start implementing these strategies today and watch your online course business thrive.

Chapter 9: Freelancing and Online Service-Based Businesses

Identifying In-Demand Freelance Skills

In today's digital age, the opportunities to make money online are endless. The rise of the gig economy and the increasing demand for remote work have made freelancing a popular choice for individuals seeking financial independence and flexibility. However, with so many options available, it can be overwhelming to determine which freelance skills are in-demand and will generate a steady income. This subchapter will guide you through the process of identifying the most sought-after skills in various niches, ensuring that you can make the most of your freelance career.

1. Make Money with Online Passive Income: When it comes to generating passive income online, skills such as affiliate marketing, content creation, search engine optimization (SEO), and email marketing are highly sought-after. These skills will enable you to create and promote profitable online businesses, such as niche websites or e-commerce stores.

2. Blogging for Profit: To monetize your blog effectively, you need to acquire skills in content writing, SEO, social media

marketing, and affiliate marketing. By mastering these skills, you can attract a large audience, generate traffic, and earn income through sponsored posts, advertisements, and affiliate partnerships.

3. E-commerce and Dropshipping: If you're interested in running an online store or dropshipping business, skills in product sourcing, branding, digital marketing, and customer service are crucial. These skills will help you identify profitable products, attract customers, and provide exceptional service to drive sales.

4. Creating and Selling Digital Products: Skills in graphic design, copywriting, video editing, and digital product creation are in high demand. By developing these skills, you can create and sell e-books, online courses, templates, and other digital products, earning passive income from your expertise.

5. Social Media Management and Marketing: As businesses increasingly rely on social media to reach their target audience, skills in social media management, content creation, community engagement, and paid advertising are invaluable. Mastering these skills will enable you to offer your services as a social media manager or marketer, helping businesses grow their online presence and increase sales.

6. Podcasting and Monetizing Audio Content: Podcasting has become a popular medium to convey information and entertain audiences. Skills in audio editing, scriptwriting, interviewing, and audience engagement are essential for creating compelling podcasts. Once you have a dedicated listener base, you can monetize your content through sponsorships, advertisements, or premium subscriptions.
7. Creating and Selling Online Courses: With the growing demand for online education, skills in course creation, curriculum design, video production, and marketing are highly sought-after. By developing these skills, you can create and sell online courses, sharing your knowledge and expertise while earning a steady income.

8. Freelancing and Online Service-based Businesses: For those interested in offering freelance services, skills such as web development, graphic design, copywriting, virtual assistance, and social media management are in high demand. By honing these skills and building a strong portfolio, you can attract clients and establish a successful online service-based business.

By identifying the in-demand freelance skills in your desired niche, you can position yourself as an expert and tap into the vast opportunities available in the online marketplace.

Whether you choose to create and sell digital products, offer freelance services, or build an online business, mastering these skills will set you on the path to financial success in the ever-evolving world of online entrepreneurship.

Setting Up Your Freelancing Business

Freelancing has emerged as a popular and lucrative way to make money online. With the freedom to work on your own terms, choose clients, and set your rates, it offers an incredible opportunity for individuals looking to make money while maintaining their independence. However, setting up a successful freelancing business requires careful planning and execution. In this subchapter, we will guide you through the essential steps to establish your freelancing business and ensure its long-term success.

Firstly, it is crucial to identify your freelancing niche. Consider your skills, experiences, and passions to determine the area in which you excel. Whether it's writing, graphic design, coding, or marketing, specializing in a particular field will help you stand out from the competition and attract high-paying clients.

Once you have identified your niche, it's time to build an online presence. Create a professional website showcasing your portfolio, skills, and services. Optimize your website for search engines to increase your visibility and attract potential clients. Additionally, establish your presence on social media platforms to network with other freelancers and potential clients.

Next, you need to set your freelancing rates. Research the market to understand the average rates in your niche and consider your experience level and the value you bring to clients. While it's important to remain competitive, avoid undervaluing your services. Quality work deserves fair compensation.

To maximize your earnings, consider diversifying your income streams. Explore opportunities for passive income such as affiliate marketing, creating and selling digital products, or blogging for profit. These additional revenue streams can provide a stable income while you build your freelancing business.

Networking is an essential aspect of freelancing. Join relevant online communities, attend industry events, and engage in conversations with like-minded professionals. Building relationships with potential clients and fellow freelancers can lead to referrals, collaborations, and new opportunities.

Finally, always prioritize professionalism in your freelancing business. Communicate clearly with clients, meet deadlines, and provide exceptional customer service. Happy clients are more likely to hire you again and recommend your services to others.

In conclusion, setting up your freelancing business requires careful planning, a strong online presence, strategic pricing, diversification of income streams, networking, and professionalism. By following these steps, you can establish a successful freelancing business and achieve your financial goals while enjoying the freedom and flexibility that freelancing offers.

Attracting and Retaining Clients as a Freelancer

As a freelancer, your success in making money online depends heavily on your ability to attract and retain clients. In this subchapter, we will explore effective strategies to help you build a loyal client base and ensure a steady stream of income in the exciting world of freelancing.

One of the most crucial aspects of attracting clients is establishing a strong online presence. Regardless of your niche, having a professional website or portfolio showcasing your skills and expertise is essential. Potential clients want to see examples of your previous work, testimonials, and contact information readily available. Utilize your website to highlight your unique selling points and differentiate yourself from the competition.

In addition to a website, leveraging social media platforms can significantly boost your online visibility. Engage with your target audience by sharing valuable content, participating in relevant communities, and showcasing your expertise. Regularly update your profiles with samples of your work, client testimonials, and case studies to effectively demonstrate your skills.
Networking is another powerful tool for attracting clients. Attend industry events, join online communities, and engage in conversations with potential clients and fellow freelancers. Building relationships and connections can lead to referrals and long-term collaborations.

Once you've attracted clients, it's crucial to focus on retaining them. Providing exceptional customer service and delivering high-quality work are essential elements of client retention. Always meet deadlines, communicate effectively, and consistently exceed expectations. Happy clients are more likely to recommend you to others and offer repeat business.

Another strategy to retain clients is by offering value-added services. Continuously develop your skills and stay on top of industry trends to provide additional services that complement your primary offering. This not only increases your value to clients but also enhances your competitive advantage.

Lastly, never underestimate the power of referrals and testimonials. Satisfied clients can become your best marketing tool. Encourage them to leave positive reviews and refer you to their networks. Offer incentives, such as discounts or freebies, to clients who refer new business to you.

In conclusion, attracting and retaining clients as a freelancer is crucial for maintaining a sustainable income stream. By establishing your online presence, leveraging social media, networking, providing exceptional service, and offering value-added services, you can build a loyal client base that will support your freelancing career for years to come.

Pricing Your Services for Profitability

In the world of online entrepreneurship, one of the key factors that determines the success of your business is how you price your services. Whether you are offering online passive income opportunities, blogging for profit, e-commerce and dropshipping, creating and selling digital products, social media management and marketing, podcasting and monetizing audio content, creating and selling online courses, or freelancing and online service-based businesses, understanding the art of pricing is crucial for profitability.

Setting the right price for your services requires a delicate balance between attracting customers and ensuring that your business remains profitable. While it may be tempting to undercut your competition and offer lower prices, this can lead to undervaluing your expertise and ultimately harming your bottom line. On the other hand, overpricing your services may deter potential customers and limit your market reach.

To determine the optimal pricing strategy, start by conducting thorough market research. Analyze your competitors' pricing, taking into account their level of expertise, quality of service, and target audience. This will give you a clear understanding of the price range in your niche and help you position yourself accordingly.

Next, consider the value that your services provide to your customers. What problem are you solving for them? How much would they be willing to pay for a solution? Understanding the perceived value of your services will allow you to price them accordingly and maximize your profitability.

Additionally, it is essential to factor in your costs and desired profit margin when setting your prices. Take into account your time, effort, and any expenses associated with delivering your services.
Consider the amount of revenue you need to generate to cover your costs and achieve your desired income goals. This will help you set realistic prices that ensure your business remains sustainable in the long run.

Lastly, don't be afraid to experiment with different pricing strategies. Consider offering different packages or tiers that cater to different customer segments. This can help you capture a wider range of customers with varying budgets and preferences.

Remember, pricing your services for profitability is a continuous process. As your business evolves and grows, regularly reassess your pricing strategy to ensure that it aligns with the value you provide and the market conditions. By mastering the art of pricing, you can maximize your profitability and build a successful online business in your chosen niche.

Scaling Your Freelancing Business and Expanding Your Service Offerings

If you are someone who wants to make money online and has chosen freelancing as your path to financial freedom, congratulations! Freelancing offers immense potential for earning a substantial income while enjoying the flexibility of working on your own terms. However, to truly maximize your earnings and build a sustainable online business, it is crucial to scale your freelancing business and expand your service offerings.

Scaling your freelancing business involves increasing your client base, income, and overall productivity. It requires strategic planning, efficient time management, and the ability to deliver exceptional results consistently. Here are some essential tips to help you scale your freelancing business successfully:

1. Define Your Niche: Identify your strengths and passions and focus on a specific niche within your chosen freelancing field. By becoming an expert in a particular area, you can attract high-paying clients who value your expertise.

2. Streamline Your Processes: Automate repetitive tasks, invest in productivity tools, and create systems that

ensure efficient project management and smooth client communication. This will free up your time to take on more clients and expand your service offerings.

3. Build a Strong Online Presence: Establish a professional website and create a compelling portfolio that showcases your skills and previous work. Utilize social media platforms to connect with potential clients and build a network of industry professionals.

4. Collaborate with Others: Consider partnering with other freelancers or online businesses to combine your skills and offer comprehensive services. This can help you tap into new markets and attract clients who require a broader range of services.

Expanding your service offerings is another critical aspect of scaling your freelancing business. By diversifying your offerings, you can cater to a wider audience and open up new streams of income. Here are some ideas to consider:

1. Upsell and Cross-sell: Identify additional services that complement your core offering and present them to your existing clients. For example, if you are a social media manager, you could offer content creation or ad campaign management services.

2. Learn New Skills: Stay updated with the latest trends and technologies in your industry and learn new skills that align with your freelancing business. For instance, if you are an e-commerce consultant, consider expanding into dropshipping or Amazon FBA.

3. Offer Consultations or Coaching: Share your expertise and knowledge by offering one-on-one consultations or coaching sessions. This can be a highly lucrative way to monetize your skills and provide personalized guidance to aspiring freelancers or online business owners.

Remember, scaling your freelancing business and expanding your service offerings require dedication, persistence, and continuous learning. By implementing these strategies and staying focused on your goals, you can turn your freelancing business into a thriving online venture that generates passive income and offers you financial freedom.

Chapter 10: Conclusion and Next Steps

Reflecting on Your Passive Income Journey

Congratulations! By reaching this point in the book, you have taken the first steps towards mastering the art of generating passive income online. As you delve deeper into the world of passive income, it is crucial to take the time to reflect on your journey and the progress you have made thus far.

For those of you who aspire to make money online, the possibilities are endless. Whether you are interested in blogging for profit, e-commerce and dropshipping, creating and selling digital products, social media management and marketing, podcasting and monetizing audio content, creating and selling online courses, or freelancing and online service-based businesses, your options are vast. However, it is essential to reflect on your chosen niche and the path you have embarked upon.

Reflecting on your passive income journey allows you to assess your goals, progress, and overall satisfaction. Take a moment to ask yourself: Are you enjoying the journey? Are you passionate about your chosen niche? Is it aligned with your skills and interests? Reflecting on these questions will help you stay motivated and focused on your ultimate goal – financial freedom.

Furthermore, reflection provides an opportunity to evaluate the strategies and techniques you have implemented. It allows you to identify what has worked well and what needs improvement. Take note of your successes and failures, as they both serve as valuable learning experiences. By reflecting on your past actions, you can make informed decisions moving forward and adjust your approach accordingly.

Additionally, reflecting on your journey helps to maintain a positive mindset. Building a passive income stream takes time and effort. It is easy to become discouraged when results do not come as quickly as expected. However, by reflecting on how far you have come and the progress you have made, you can celebrate your achievements, no matter how small. This positive mindset will motivate you to persevere through challenges and setbacks, ultimately leading you to success.

In conclusion, reflecting on your passive income journey is a vital component of your success. It allows you to assess your goals, evaluate your strategies, and maintain a positive mindset.

Remember, making money online is a journey, and every step forward counts. So, take the time to reflect, celebrate your achievements, and continue moving towards financial freedom.

Setting Goals and Taking Action

In order to achieve success in the world of online passive income, it is crucial to set clear goals and take consistent action towards achieving them. This subchapter will guide you through the process of setting effective goals and provide valuable insights on how to take decisive action to turn your dreams into reality.

When it comes to making money online, it's important to have a clear vision of what you want to achieve. Setting specific and measurable goals allows you to stay focused and motivated throughout your journey. Whether your goal is to make $1,000 per month through blogging, create and sell digital products, or become a successful social media manager, defining your objectives is the first step towards success.

Once you have set your goals, it's time to take action. Taking consistent and strategic action is the key to turning your dreams into a profitable reality. Start by breaking down your larger goals into smaller, actionable steps. For instance, if your goal is to make $1,000 per month through blogging, your action steps could include writing and publishing three high-quality blog posts per week, promoting your content on social media platforms, and monetizing your blog through affiliate marketing or sponsored posts.

It's important to hold yourself accountable and stay disciplined in your actions. Consistency is key in building a successful online passive income stream. Commit to a schedule and stick to it. Treat your online business as a real business, dedicating specific hours each day or week to work towards your goals.

Additionally, it's crucial to continuously educate yourself and stay updated on the latest trends and strategies in your chosen niche. Attend webinars, read books, and join relevant online communities to gain valuable insights and stay ahead of the competition.

Remember, success rarely happens overnight. It takes time, effort, and perseverance to build a profitable online business. Celebrate small wins along the way and use any setbacks as learning opportunities to refine your strategies and improve your results.

In conclusion, setting goals and taking consistent action

are essential steps towards achieving financial success in the online world. Define your objectives, break them down into actionable steps, stay disciplined, and continuously educate yourself. By doing so, you'll be well on your way to mastering the art of making money online through various passive income streams.

Continuously Learning and Adapting in the Online Passive Income World

In the rapidly evolving world of online passive income, where trends and technologies change at the blink of an eye, one must embrace the mindset of continuous learning and adaptation to stay ahead of the curve. This subchapter delves into the importance of staying updated and agile in various niches such as making money with online passive income, blogging for profit, e-commerce and dropshipping, creating and selling digital products, social media management and marketing, podcasting and monetizing audio content, creating and selling online courses, as well as freelancing and online service-based businesses.

For individuals seeking to make money online, it is crucial to understand that success is not a one- time achievement but a constant journey. The strategies and techniques that worked yesterday may not yield the same results tomorrow. Therefore, it becomes imperative to continuously learn and adapt to the ever-changing landscape of online passive income. This subchapter provides valuable insights and practical tips on how to keep up with the latest trends and developments in each niche.

Whether you are interested in blogging for profit, e-commerce, or dropshipping, this subchapter emphasizes the importance of staying updated with the latest SEO practices, understanding consumer behavior, and leveraging emerging technologies to drive traffic and boost sales. It also explores the world of creating and selling digital products, highlighting the significance of market research, content creation, and effective marketing strategies.

Moreover, for those interested in social media management and marketing, podcasting and monetizing audio content, creating and selling online courses, or freelancing and online service-based businesses, this subchapter offers insights into harnessing the power of social media platforms, building a loyal audience, monetizing content, and providing value in a competitive market.

In conclusion, the online passive income world is a dynamic and ever-changing landscape. To succeed in this realm, individuals must embrace lifelong learning, adapt to emerging trends, and continuously refine their strategies.

Whether you are a blogger, e-commerce entrepreneur, content creator, social media manager, or freelancer, this subchapter equips you with the knowledge and tools necessary to thrive in your niche. So, dive into the world of continuous learning and adaptation, and unlock the potential of online passive income.

All or some of the content of this ebook has been generated with the assistance of ChatGPT, an AI language model developed by OpenAI. While efforts have been made to provide accurate and reliable information, the ebook should not be considered a substitute for professional advice or expertise.

www.ingramcontent.com/pod-product-compliance
Lightning Source LLC
Chambersburg PA
CBHW072131270726

48661CB00018BA/1543